WOMAN'S WORK

For Rosemary Zins,

Hope you enjoy this!

WOMAN'S WORK

With all best wishes from the author.

Eleanor M. Imperato

Eleanor M. Imperato
Manhasset, NY
March 16, 2011

KILIMA HOUSE PUBLISHERS
NEW YORK

Published in the United States of America 2008 by
Kilima House Publishers
P.O. Box 1057
Manhasset, NY 11030

Some of these poems previously appeared in the following publications, to whose editors grateful acknowledgment is made: *Beyond the Horizon, La Sarta, Manhasset Press.*

Designed by Brigid McCarthy
Photos by Chris Lopez

Printed on acid free paper

Library of Congress Control Number: 2008925420

ISBN: 978-0-910385-04-6

Manufactured in the United States of America

Lovingly dedicated to

Pat

Alison

Gavin

Austin

who are at once my universe

and my cocoon

Contents

ON MY OWN

You Are Not Me

Foreword

WOMAN'S WORK is an apt and provocative title for this collection of poems, reinforcing the female sensibility so clearly at work in these pages, and pointing out, not without irony, the enduring power of gentleness. The title poem focuses on the contrast between male surge and female grace, concluding that while the former is clearly showier (and noisier), the latter embodies the life force itself, nutritive and long-lasting.

Imperato's book covers a lot of ground, chronologically, geographically, and emotionally. We experience the visions of children, adolescents, young lovers, and old people. We move through the present and the past seamlessly, touched as much by the mourning woman a century away in "My Man, He Went A-Whaling" as by the fulfilled modern day wife in "Bread and Roses." We travel to Italy, Turkey, Alaska, Iceland, England. We move through loneliness, joy, desire, grief, hope. We examine rural life, urban disaster, the simple fulfillment of cooking for loved ones, the poignant beauty of the Iditarod champions.

Many of the poems in this volume are portraits. We read about the lives of a spoiled child, a lonely young woman, an appreciative wife, a loving mother, a disoriented grandmother, a sailor's widow ("her young sons in her wake"). Only some of these are personae of the poet. The others are drawn from Imperato's finely tuned observations of family, friends, strangers, and created characters. The people we read about seem as connected to us as they are to the author, each representative of an aspect of ourselves. In this way, *Woman's Work* reminds me of Sherwood Anderson's *Winesburg, Ohio,* another book full of intriguing characters with whom we quickly feel intimate.

When not exploring the range and depth of her characters, Imperato turns her attention to important personal, social, and philosophical issues, metaphorically asking many significant questions: What are the limits of the mother/daughter relationship? What is the shape of grief? How are women all over the world viscerally connected? What is the meaning of love in the face of death? What is the meaning of death in the face of love? The reader is not tempted to question her choice of subject matter since the book coheres in an almost mysterious way, weaving family scenes with international observations, personal anecdotes with eerie fantasies. Imperato questions herself, those around her, even God, with a determination to understand and accept all that life offers and denies. Clearly, doing so is hard work.

Woman's Work, like so many musical pieces, is organized into three sections. Indeed, it reads like a piece of music, smooth and amazingly lyrical. Images rise in Imperato's mind, and then in ours, from the rhythms of the kitchen, the sewing room, the garden, the stars, and, frequently, the sea. She is a true poet, bound to the sound as well as the meaning of her words. Examples of her lyricism abound: "to ride the waves like sleighs on snow," "holding our grief like ripe persimmons," "my (fishing) line flirts gently through the liquid stillness," "waves of desert lapping at your doorstep," "dervish blizzards," "a shawl of silence," and "swollen flanks of smoke dark sky/pregnant with the night." Throughout the book, the poet winds her "tendrils of poetry" delicately, gracefully, creating new growth as she goes.

Woman's work is, proverbially, never done. In this collection, we never want it to be. Better to savor the poems included here, those that bring a chill as well as those that provide warmth, than to have to leave the world of longings and imaginings the poet creates for us. Like her mother, the seamstress, Imperato sews her words together precisely, elegantly, with wonderful strength and durability, artistry in every stitch.

Susan Astor

Acknowledgments

CREATION is never a solitary art. While it was my pen that transmitted my thoughts and feelings onto paper, I owe a tremendous debt of gratitude to many people.

First on the list is my wonderful husband of thirty years, Pat. He has witnessed my womanhood in all its facets and has encouraged me to fulfill all the dreams and passions of my life. He is truly my anchor, steady as our tides ebb and flow. A simple thank you is not enough, but the love that I hold for him should suffice for the rest of our days. The closeness I share with my children is priceless, each of them has enriched my life beyond measure. Alison shares the doubts, the depths, the privileges, and the frustrations of woman's work; Gavin can match my intellectual and philosophical flights of fancy: classical, modern, and post-modern; Austin's laconic demeanor hides a passionate, artistic vein that I have been allowed to glimpse and admire. Thank you for nurturing me.

Susan Astor, friend, poet, and author of *Spider Lies*, has lovingly tended the blossoming of my own poetry. Her encouragement, her critiques, and her uncanny gift for finding the strength of a poem beneath the flowery verbiage, have been invaluable. The creative support and friendship of fellow poets Mary Jane Peterson, Mary Watts, Anne Bohlin, Muriel Weinstein, Rosalind Chaikin, and Richard Barnhart are welcome and treasured.

Thank you to Chris Lopez, good friend and gifted photographer. I have always admired her work and I am proud to have her photos illustrating this volume. Heartfelt thanks are extended to Brigid McCarthy, designer of books for Kilima House Publishers and other publishers. Her artistry in layout and design are outstanding, as is her patience with all the fine details of production. I also wish to thank Leonard Kahan for his assistance in scanning the photographs.

Camille Dee, a dear and steadfast friend, was very generous with her time and her sharp skills in proofing the manuscript. I thank her profusely. To Inge Castrissiades, longtime friend and "woman, just like me," my sincere thanks for her friendship and support.

To my sisters Toni and Patricia, who were the first readers and critics of my poetry, deep and loving thanks for their unwavering faith in my writing abilities.

Finally, a sad farewell to Mary Whitney, friend of countless days, who has heard the cadence of my poems, not with her senses, but with her heart.

Eleanor M. Imperato

CYCLES

Cycles

in a distant dream
I feel the warm wet walls
of my mother's womb
the tender stroking
of her hand
against the tight drum
of her belly

I hear the plaintive chorus
of a lullaby and
the muffled bass line
of her heart
somersaults in my liquid bed
send ripples of smiles
to her tired young face

now like my mother
I feel the leaps of my
unborn child
its hiccups
punctuate my
soporific afternoons
a dream
almost
become reality

August Heat

grandfather and I sleep
on cool canvas cots
breathing slow

August heat
seeps unwelcome
through tight-lipped shutters
slivers of sun insinuate themselves
into the daytime darkness of the room

the world lies still
in the forever hours
of a summer afternoon
only the droning of a bee
weaves trance-like cobwebs
round our heads

sinuous clouds of fragrant coffee
stir our senses
rouse us to the distant chatter
of china cups and spoons

That Summer Day

The leaves were silent, overcome by heat,
the lizards wary, in their stone-like stance,
while coins of sunlight, strewn among the rocks,
filtered the dancing dust motes in the air.

The path was narrow, the world wide to me,
my hand was safe in his too trembling grasp,
as old and young, our steps moved slow, to reach
the crumbled relics of an unknown war.

The pallid colors of a frescoed Virgin
stood in the open air, amidst a nave
of golden grass burdened by the sun,
and lonely poppies with their heads bowed low.

The murmured prayers of lethargic bees
easily mingled with our quiet breaths
as he and I stood still, till dusk set in,
in that burned-out shrine, on that summer day.

The war forgotten, my grandfather gone,
the grass plowed under, and the poppies crushed,
there are no memories in the summer air,
only the magic in my secret heart.

Winter Evening

mushrooms sizzle in a pan
sibilant wags
whisper secrets
filling the sudden blackness
of the room

wind snaps wires
the feeble light
encircling
our expectant table
fails

hot coals in a brazier
cradled in soft beds
of ash
sputter their displeasure
as grandfather prods them
into wakefulness

their warm sighs
rise
reluctantly
into the winter chill
as we wait for supper
in darkness
softened
by a candle's breath

Almost a Man

your dimpled chin
made the obstetric nurses smile
but as I nursed you in our private corner
I touched your ear lobe
crinkled, dog-eared
like my favorite book
I'd always know you in a crowd

you never liked the crowds
but were content
constructing plows from cardboard
and an endless roll of tape
your sister would have traded you
for pennies, yet you pranced
not knowing, by her side

how then, did you become
almost a man
not quite at peace with
the uneven cadence of your life
whitewater rushing
over boulders in a stream
I look beyond the stubble on your chin
and wonder when the turbulence
becomes serenity

even in the solemnity of night
I see your not-so-compact body
tangled in the sheets
jostling the woven red and yellow trucks
the threadbare remnants of your childhood

River Run

like your brother
you run the rapids
of your adolescence
follow a swift descent
through gaping canyons
past rock-studded shores
angry waters bullying your boat

like a ghost rudder
I sit astern
calling out dangers, urging caution
while you steer your uncertain course
I do not aid your journey
merely confound your judgment

I am the vestige of my own currents
already spent
safe at harbor
I have no place aboard your craft

Guitar Man

you listen, look sideways
absorb life askance
few words escape your lips

third child, used to waiting
for your turn
you now step back
choose your solitude
retreat into
a world of sound

your feelings strum
the chords of your guitar
meld with the thrumming
of a bass
pound with the rock-hot
pulse of drums
only you can hear

Firefly Girl

they will easily span an octave
I smiled
as your long and graceful fingers
curled round my breast
oblivious to my joy
your eager cheeks
filled with the first taste of life

music lulled you to reluctant rest
set the cadence of your days
with a tick-tock clock
that never stopped
and a toy turtle snapping
at your heels all day

at play you were the queen
your brothers pawns   dispensable
friends were court or minions
as your whim desired

you painted portraits
of your regal face
not with the lustrous brown
of your hair and eyes
but with imagined locks
of sungold strands
and seablue eyes

in the summer dusk
of your backyard forest
you softly stroked
a hard cicada's back
her tired wings fluttered
one last lingering flight

you gathered fireflies
in a transparent universe of glass
constellations of stars
glowing
as you slept

firefly girl
proud at last of your sable hair
of the jewel brilliance of your dark dark eyes
searching for paths
out of a childhood garden

What is it, Daughter

that keeps you under
the shadow of a man
cowered and caged
afraid to seek the sun
to run across the grass
into your life's horizon?

I see the shadow deepen
blur the fireglow in your eyes
shutter your dreams against the light
as your longings settle
like dust upon a table

step into the light   woman
wipe the cobwebs from your brow
sing joy into your limbs
waken your dreams

Resplendent Beggar

you hold a patient vigil
by the pantry door
haunches folded neatly
over your back paws
front legs like columns
framing your perfect body
bright green eyes staring
at any who dare
look in your direction
ears at the ready, crown
on your feline head
there is no need for miaows
we know you beg
for treats, shameless
in your quiet persistence
white silk and gray fur
shimmering at rest
in one fluid pose

Tiger

my day began with you:

your feline prayers, rusty hinges
on the doors of dawn

wake me, open my eyes
to the chill air of another day

I touch soft fur, scented with your
bed partner's musk

your gray markings, white and pink
smile framed by whiskers

sphinx-like poses, wanton
stretchings, paw caresses,

I, your slave, bend, hoist your
not insubstantial body

to the kitchen sink, where the cool,
running stream is your delight

no longer limber, you and I
stretch beyond our means

vitamins for me, thyroid drops for you
just to get us through our day

your narcotizing sleep curled in
a gray-white loaf, waiting

my thousand keyboard strokes,
office e-motions without meaning

at dusk, as I reenter my domain
you, regal sentinel, welcome me

for our forebearance, and at last
free from loneliness

we share treats, turkey for you,
roasted almonds for me

then you supervise my cooking,
tasting crumbs, licking sauces

at dinner you are happy
on a purloined chair, displacing

the master of the house,
he does not mind

thyroid drops again, tuna-flavored
life-nourishing cat-candy

like a baby, though you are
octogenarian, you claim

my lap as our old bones
sink in an old armchair

watch the flickers of
our favorite shows

before bedtime, as I read
my books, again you steal

my space, this time it is
I who must displace you

as we drift together
into our separate dreams

you linger yet, warming
me still with memories

Bread and Roses

on this the 27th eve
of our life together
you hold as gifts
pale cream roses
with a touch of blush
around their crowns

one for each of us
you   me
Alison   Gavin   Austin
even Tiger our
beloved furry baby
rounds out our family bouquet

with mischief in your eyes
you then reveal
a dark walnut-studded
raisin-starred
loaf of peasant bread

you smile
at my eagerness to
savor it like a child

my life is full
now and tomorrow
you nourish me
completely

Woman's Work

in the garage father and son
rev up the engine
ready to plunge
into the snow

sprays of crackling ice
spew out
of a gaping mouth
like profanities

at the back door
mother and daughter
wait for the last snowflake
to settle
on the ice sparkled yews

gently with soft gloved hands
they brush crowns and limbs
free of burdening snow

smile as they see branches
stretch awake
limber again

Vespers

olive oil and garlic
parsley   fresh tomatoes
stir
coax a thick sauce to life
add chicken breasts
simmer till the fork
finds no resistance from the flesh

shred the lettuce
endive
radicchio
toss with oil
no vinegar no lemon
sweeter taste

steam in a basket
a vegetarian bouquet
set the table
slice the semolina bread

sit   wait
for the children husband
to return
steal a moment
reach for a book
never far away

Winds of Freedom

read by the author
at the Bryn Mawr College Convocation
May 13, 2000

when first you joined our lives
your world was our embrace
love's breath the warmth of life

as time went by
the winds of freedom
sang the siren songs
of discovery and knowledge

faint breezes
whispered in your hair
of secret coves
beyond the cliffs
we marveled at your joy

the sometimes gales
of teenage years
darkened your horizon
wreaked havoc
on our aging compass

gusts took you on a
whirlwind tour of life
we kept the beacon burning

now we stand on shore
proud of your endurance
your sails unfurled
billowing with hope
filled with
the winds of freedom

La Sarta

The Seamstress

she sits there at first light
last light
and far into the night
head down
shoulders bent
hands sailing on a sea of silk
she cuts the lace just so
one rose then two
then more and more
the petals float
like foam atop the waves

her perfect stitches
measure
daylights
nightlights
until the wedding dawn arrives

hands at anchor
head upturned
she sees the eyes of her firstborn bride
look down
through a mist of tears
at the clouds of white
gathered near her heart

she feels the warmth of
memory rise

when smoke of war was in the air
and peace was still to come
she walked down the aisle of an ancient church
in a gown her hands had wrought
from tulle and satin soft and rare

Dried Flowers

you ask
in a plaintive   wistful voice
if I tend to my garden
I reply that it is winter

you press me further

are the lilac trees in bloom?

you hear the words I use
to paint the snow and ice
that silence life outside my door
but in your mind
dogwood petals glow
roses blush in sunlight

pity, it was a lovely garden

mother, do you understand
that spring may never come again
and that the only blossoms
I may tend
are those you
carefully preserved
prolonging beauty
if not life?

don't you like flowers anymore?

Coma

I do not see you
lying there at night
forgotten by the callous nurses
who in their brusque Italian tones
already count you
among the dead

nor do I see your lips
quiver as a drop of water
nestles in the corner of your mouth

an ocean lies between us
as it has done for years

my sister hopes
the miracle of waking is
at hand
she urges me to talk to you
as she places the phone
next to your ear
I am to comfort you
with a virtual embrace

dutifully I proclaim my love

the nurses must be right
you do not answer
and the small twitch
my sister mistakes
for consciousness
is just a flicker

Hiding Out

she sits in an empty closet
eyes shut
dank hair spilling on thin arms
that frame
blood-embroidered knees

darkness is comfort
for a while at least

she knows the game
will end
when the door opens to the light
when the next refuge
will be
in her mother's arms

she hears no footfalls
nor the crisp sound of her name
time holds its breath
darkness becomes mud
that fills her mouth
immures her eyes
binds her feet

because
she knows
this is no longer play
she settles into
darkness

Midnight

I am not quite asleep
the phone rings
my sister's voice from half a world away
whispers
Mother died this morning, just a little while ago
not unexpected, it sounds like news

adrenalin kicks in
must catch a flight to Naples
ask for bereavement leave at work
pack light, it's early summer
lovely time in Italy
first I must sleep

sleep? my mother died
she died, what does that mean?
she won't ever sew my clothes again?
she hasn't done so in years
she won't ever answer the phone again?

I live here, she lives there
lived
everything must be past tense
from now on

for months
I dreaded phone calls
in the night, now I can sleep
yes, sleep, she sleeps
no, *she died*

my sisters say I will arrive in time
for mass before the burial
they will wait for me
my plane is late, so late
I miss connections
spend all day
at the airport in Rome
shuttle from one counter
to another
pleading with the airport staff
my mother died
I must get on this plane
there is no kindness
we are sorry

I'm being punished
I know
I always said I'd never go to her funeral
I couldn't bear her absence
I would grieve at home

this is real now
I want to be there
in church
I want to cry
with them, my sisters
my uncles, my cousins

I want to be there when
the earth covers her coffin
I want to feel the weight of loss

instead I wait
I cry alone and without shame
as travelers pass by me
waiting is all that I can do

my sisters bury Mother without me
they do not wait
it is dark when I arrive
at Mother's house
hers no longer

she used to wait for me

Cemetery Walk

I
three daughters, sisters
come to mourn our mother
holding our grief
like ripe persimmons
soft sun globes cradled
in our hands
we walk on cobbled streets among
marble chapels, mausoleums
rooted to the vanities of earth

II
clusters of lilies, carnations, gladioli
pose languidly against the walls
heavily rouged harlots at a funeral
one can so easily mistake the stench
of rotting flowers
for decomposing flesh
skylarks sing descants of life
as they flutter against
the translucent sapphire
of a summer sky

III
we round a corner
pass a field of small white tombstones
palm fronds braided into crosses
rise like sentinels from their
brown-crusted base
pale, wilted roses sadly speak
of lives that never bloomed
we are children searching for
our mother's plot
among rough, narrow alleys
until we reach the terraced gardens
of the newly dead

27

IV
there in a corner, alone
in a fallow strip of land
we find our mother's place at last
stray dogs scamper
lap water from an ancient faucet
eat pasta scraps
remnants of a groundskeeper's feast
from bowls cracked by time
on soil that holds eternity in its womb

V
out of the depths of a just dug grave
rise the staccato yelps of a rascal puppy
a caretaker leans prone into the hole
his dirt stained fingers
clutch the errant scruff
set it free to find
its mother

VI
yesterday's burial left a
makeshift cross over a mound of earth
heaps of blossoms already fading
under the strong southern sun
we clear withered leaves
fill buckets with cool water
arrange flowers, tidy this
last earthly corner of our mother's life

VII
over her heart, or where we think
her heart should be
we lay three small bouquets
messages of love
that will receive no answer
still, we each cull
one bloom as we imagine
a last *I love you*
from her lips

VIII
tears bind us, sisters
heads bent in prayer
holding hands around this grave
this temporary place, until the gruesome custom
of symbolic resurrection
a year, two years hence
when those who tend the graves
strip her bones clear of her once soft skin
of the woman muscles that bore us into life

IX
the remnant scaffolds of her body
will not rest alone
in the forever dark of a crypt of stone
but as she wished
in an apartment house of death
with her spouse, in a marble niche
a choice location with a view
that overlooks for all eternity
sea light on the Naples bay

Good Mother, Bad Mother

while I watched behind a chair
you gave away my baby clothes
the ones you sewed, embroidered
with your *golden hands*
those less fortunate than I
needed them more, you said

was there also need to give away
my red silk skirt, rich and
redolent of Spain?

your love was manifest
in stitches
yet you unraveled it

at your suggestion, when
I grew to womanhood
ready to become a bride
I gathered letters
from my youthful loves
tore them into pieces
threw my past away

never convinced that I was loved
they would have been proof

you did love me, didn't you?
when dawn found you
huddled near the stove
threading the last needle
finishing a special dress or coat
to be worn that very day

you did love me, didn't you?
when you fashioned
pressed flowers
portraits of my garden
when your last thoughts
were of my dogwoods
and my roses

Mother

you who are buried
in the soft womb of earth
know what lies between
the nothingness of winter
and the renaissance of spring
dormancy   a folding-in of self
before the blooms burst forth

are you then asleep   Mother
within the dark embrace of death
waiting to awake
into the light of heaven
like hyacinths in the sun?

or is your flesh spent
void of life flow
crumpled   wilted
like the roses on your grave?
have your bones
settled in a jumbled heap
at one with clay and gravel
soon to wash away
with snows and rains
of time?

where are you, Mother?

if you are in heaven
do you see me
mirror image of your life
hemming my daughter's skirt
breathing hot vapors from an iron
as I smooth wrinkles in unruly fabric?

do you see me
anguished
not to have bid goodbye
not to have touched your hand
not to have heard those words
you left unsaid
that now could
salve my pain   move me
to accept your death?

where are you, Mother?

In My Night Table

among the scented nightgowns
I find a letter in your small, round hand
forgotten
almost a decade old it sleeps, unopened
under my unseeing eyes

I scan its contents
remember my request
that prompted your reply
and my safekeeping

be pleased with
how I write and how
I express myself
you say and then begin
the story of your life

a young girl
not too fond of school
but skilled with lace
passionate with sewing
a timid bride who
although at risk of death
from childbirth
joyfully welcomed
her first daughter
then another
and another still
just before sailing
for an alien land

suffering and sacrifice
warp and woof of your unsung talents
creativity subsumed to mother-love
that speaks
through the silent
melody of death

I have my answers, Mother.

ON MY OWN

On My Own

Summer 1973

eyelids of lavender and green
soft coral lips
golden rings   rose petal scent
8:19   two turns of the key   the world
stale air   heavy air
a face to the city   young and sad

steps to the human stage
the same streets   the same bricks
the same engines   monotony
creeping over asphalt on its rubber feet
if senses can be dulled existence can be borne

workers whistle
as I pass   I do not welcome
reminders of my womanly appeal

what does it matter to me
if the birds sing
in harmony with the wind
today
when I decide to spin
a web around my heart
a cocoon   just the right size?

the world is a precarious place
so down into the underground
every life day   every day
jarred by impulses of destruction
no exits once the wheels start reeling

the ritual never ends
random flashes of communication
run an obstacle course to the mind
the give and take   never giving   never taking

5:30 the men are still there
gazing down at the wounds
they have cut in the earth

I wonder why the warm
soft lights and the hushed
feel of the ground
remind me of wars
I never saw

the key turns clockwise
my silent companions await
greet me with patient inertia

everything in order   the plants are still alive

Quiet Child

I was a quiet child
my mother always said
so quiet that often
she forgot me
in the garden
there in the stroller
looking at the lemon trees
listening to the sparrows

as I grew up
I read quietly for hours
waves of words engulfed me
rendered mute my own

when you marry, how will you care
for your children, always your head
in a book?

I am no longer quiet
and have children of my own
trees make my heart rejoice
but a book
is still a siren song

Courtyard Bully

on a flat stone slab
in my grandmother's courtyard
I sit, alone
a toy dog by my side
weaving a daisy chain
of ivy vines and clover

fragile still from fever and bronchitis
through the hoarseness of my voice
I breathe in summer
spiced with lemon scent
from ripe yellow ovals
nestled in a weave of deep green gloss

a harem of bored hens
scratch the hard-packed soil
look up for a moment
as a rooster struts
feathers and comb puffed out
crowing his manly pride

in sudden rage he flies straight to my perch
his talons dig into my thin child's chest
his beak pecks right between my eyes
warm blood trickles on my lips
his malicious declarations
drown out my raspy cry of pain

rescue comes swiftly
as my mother spies
the flurry of wings from a kitchen window
my grandmother vows
to pluck him, season him, simmer him
in the most flavorful of Sunday stews

First Time Fish

yellow perch
        swishing
in the blue
        steel water
curious
        at the glittering fin
darting coyly
        toward the sun
hunger pulls you to me
        or the lure of
joyous chase
        my line flirts
gently
        through the
liquid stillness
        as my rod stands straight
I wait
        for the tell-tale tug
                reel me in
my first time fish
        I reel you in
like a first time love
        perfect and sublime

Tidal Wave

locked in this position
my job   my nine to five security
I can forget you for an hour or two
and for an hour or two
believe the world is right
you are just another someone in my life

once the pressure breaks
a tidal wave of you
surges   engulfs me
fills all the sculptured crags
within my mind
then leaves me
naked
like eroded cliffs
while the frothing violence
ebbs

Island in the Sun

images have gone and so have
      written notes
I kept no traces of your outward life

I have destroyed the obvious
      yet
I can't forget
      the pouring of the rain
      the gravel on the path
      the waves
      the steel drums
      the wind

my life has gone contemporary now
the walls are new
      the paint still fresh
I'm growing crystal flowers
      painting silk-screens in my mind

I can't forget
      the breath of dawn
      upon your naked body
I can't forget the silence
      of your heart

stepping back I watch
      my shadow move
Sunday-city
      just the living of the bricks
I'm all alone
and all I said
      was no

Waiting for the Call

no rings
all is quiet
quieter than I wish
I hear the silence of a voice
not near   not wired
heavy time
stiller than the stagnant mind
cigarettes and ashes
colorless smoke
vanishing hours
moments of fears
moments of love
moments of
ah
there you are

Listening to Mozart's Horn Concerto

after the enveloping torpor
of a shuttered room
liberation
the sudden thrust into the open air
the trumpet's crescendo echoes
lifting me
to that mysterious place
where light and love reside
that other world
where touching you
transforms the tangible to the eternal
where togetherness
is counterpoint
and perfect harmony
the music swells
the heart swells
but without you
there is no radiance

Waiting in Istanbul

suspended
between the gardens of Shiraz
and the woods of Hampstead Heath

I am waiting
waiting
in the waiting lounge
en route
to where my spirit anchors
spent   searching
for my ancient dreams

I sit   cornered in sterility
molding myself
into the molded plastic

waiting

there are no souks to while the hours
to tempt with gold and fool the heart
as I wait
upon this Turkish soil
Turkish soil   not a Turkish soul in sight

I sit
waiting
in the waiting lounge

I've been where women
wear their veils and
speak with moving eyes

I've been where men's old cunning
is hidden
in their sheep-curled hair

I've been where past has
not yet reached today
and where today
is where
tomorrow ought to be

still   I sit
waiting

Perfect English Afternoon

we sat for hours
on a chintz-covered sofa
pillows at our back
silence blooming in the dusk
oppressive as the scent of roses
just outside the window
masses of large pink-petaled heads
cocked in expectant poses
listening

the sun projected shadows
black and gold on striped
green satin walls
we sipped our sherry slowly
let it soothe our sleeping tongues

you at one end I at the other
we should have been entwined
like the roses on the trellis

you said
I should have known
the reason for your silence

I did not know
I did not ask

Iceman

you've always been old
a lover with an iceberg core
fjordlike   crystal cut
reaches of your mind
burst clouds
knife water

what can fill
your impenetrable crags?

I saw you crying the other day
perhaps you felt me
joining your despair
perhaps you faced yourself
as just another man

how can I breach the moat
around your heart?

touch   sight   words
they fail
I have to move away
to make room
for your shrinking world

your smile belies
the torment of your life
I see the embers
the spent existence of a boy
not grown to manhood

I do not want to save you
I do not want you changed
I do not want your life

I want
knowledge shared
currents flowing
iron melting

51

A Time to Weed

this much I know:
for every joy
that comes into my life
there are a hundred sorrows
I must endure

unbidden weeds
they fill the cracks
between the bricks
tough roots
commandeering space
where there is no
space to spare

I kneel in pain
grieve as my tears
water new sprouts
that buckle bricks
menace the even
conduct of my path

this much I know:
grief gives way to anger
as determined fingers
scrape the rough surface
curl round the earthen root
pull the reluctant crown
gloat with the blood of victory

Obsession

deep rooted weed
hardy, tenacious, green
even though
it hides far into the shade
in a corner of my garden

nourished by rain
and what it will accept of sun
blooms in season
dies back when earth is cold

I tend my beds
uproot its cousins
but let *it* stand

pulling it would break my heart

Burdens

My verse represents a handle I can grasp in
Order not to yield to the centrifugal forces which
Are trying to throw me off the world.

— OGDEN NASH

Throw me off the world, I do not have the strength it takes
to hold on to poems. Like ghosts they hover
around the fringes of my consciousness. I see them,
not just with my mind's eye, but for what they truly are:
insubstantial things, born of some unknown desire.

How can I grasp them when there is no fixed point
from which I can steady my hand? Everything moves,
everything precariously perched on the edge
of an abyss. Let the centrifugal force
spin me out into the void, among the stars,
into nothingness, where time slows to a standstill,
where pain loses its incessant beating.

Let other hands grasp those ghosts,
what are they to me? Unformed beings,
burdens, light-bearing burdens, too bright to bear.
My eyes shut them out.

Black Hole

You must write about that feeling.
Do not squeeze it inside.
— YEVGENY YEVTUSHENKO

I am an expert trapper

energy flows inside me
           light
           matter
           particles
swirl in a tight embrace of
           force
           strength
           gravity
that pulls inward
           hope
           despair
           joy
into a globe of infinite density

the brilliance of a star
           shrinking
           collapsing
           centering
all light into my dark heart

I Smuggle a Stuffed Puffin from Iceland

I stalk him among the rock ledges
through warms pools of seawater
edging closer
careful not to squelch under my boots
the slippery bursas of seaweed

his eyes laser me with a calculated sneer ·
oblivious to the angry skuas
practicing flybys above our heads

camera ready I raise the lens
frame the shot
wait for the perfect moment
as dreams of *National Geographic* glory
make my shutter quiver

tired of my indecision
with a fulminating glance
he flies away

miffed at my loss
I seek redress at tourist shops
there he stands on a dusty shelf
same haughty pose
though his beak has lost
its brilliance
victim of a not-so-sporting chase

I do not haggle, but bag him
hide him in my coat

it is unseemly for a
nature lover to indulge in
stuffed dead birds

Pagan Dream

in the cathedral cave
of my desire
an ancient woman
sits
framed by firelight
her tinder eyes
burn
through my wooden stance
beckon
my compliance
for you   she whispers
coal black sleeves
unfold   reveal
a gilded book
a rough-hewn cross
gifts of faith
faith in my gifts

Islands

because you are exotic
inaccessible lands
in a too crowded world

because you are
infinitesimal specks
on blue Atlantic waters

St. Helena
Ascension
Tristan da Cunha

because you are
wind-ravaged at the crossroads
of untamable forces

because your wildlife
outnumbers human life
lives in scripted, cruel harmony

South Georgia
Falklands
Marion Island

I hear your call

Speak to Me, Silence of the Arctic

I who am afraid of night

look clear-eyed into this dark expanse
at once sea ice and blue-black sky
not yet burdened by the dawn
                    boundless, beyond time

a raven flies above me
                    soundless
through the cold dry air
shadows an Alaskan husky
loping surefooted
through the snowdrifts

at the still point of being
I stare into eternity
let it invade me with
                    its dark, stark beauty

speak to me, Silence,
                    tell me
what secrets am I to understand?

Dusk on the Bering Sea

forgetting the city at my back
the warm pot of reindeer stew
the smooth silk feel of an ivory tusk
the howl of a dog's unrest

I stand with feet bound to the snow
the ice that covers deep dark water
my arms outstretched
to rim the breadth
of its brooding mystery

a veil of fog rises
into the still white air
deepens into shades of pearl
blurs the horizon
sea and sky lock
into a chill embrace

overwhelmed with joy
I feel no cold
I feel no fear

Iditarod Champion

 alone in the enormity of sky
his feeble head lamp
casts a muted light
upon the frost-brushed coats
of huskies on the run

 dark shadows on a dark night
dogs   musher sled
one undulating wave
chasing impatient miles
to the bright lights of town

 at his back, forgotten,
wind-lashed whiteouts
knife-slitting cold
tangled tug lines
icy runs on a river bed

 finally, up a steep rise
off the ice of the Bering coast
through shouting crowds
down the snow-packed chute
to the burled arch of Nome

Victory!

 cheers crackle the frozen air
snap icicles that cling
to the stiff moustache
of the musher champion

 a ruff of roses sits
round the lead dog's neck
his sleep-filled eyes
dreaming of a warm straw bed

Racers at Rest

straw pallets
strung like amber ovals
on a white velvet sea
glow warm in a pool of light
under a navy sky

you fill these cradles
curl yourselves in
tight circles of fur
burrow your weary bodies
in round hollows of warmth

from time to time
one of you howls
another raises a head
and with a raspy, wet tongue
brushes ice needles from sore paws
your human handlers walk quietly
through this open air nursery
soothe the sleepless
with a gentle ear rub
add more straw   fill food bowls

from a bluff above you
I see your dreams hover
like fog mists from the sea:
Iditarod runs through icy rivers
sled runners hissing behind you
dervish blizzards slowing you down

I feel your lungs expand
with crystal air
your sweaty tongues
hanging engorged
as your muscles burn
under the blinding sun
framed by cobalt skies

humbled by your canine grace
I whisper softly
good night, doggies

Cove Drive

the hill is steep, I measure
      heartbeats, lungbreaths, as I climb
            weighed down by thoughts of
                  unmade beds and breadcrumbs
                        on the kitchen floor

midmorning solace, on a quiet
      suburban road, only the birds
            trade gossip on the fly
                  from oak to spruce
                        to sycamore

branches quiver, leaves
      meander as they fall,
            languid ladies on an autumn stroll
                  clad in red, rust, brown, and amber
                        coated with a wash of gold

as the hill rises, so my eyes
      reach up into a perfect round
            of sky, cobalt blue framed by clouds
                  of shocking white, a roundel in
                        an open air cathedral

my cadence falters, I stand still
      breathe in the sharp incense
            of fall, gasp at the glimpse
                  of heaven, bed burdens lifted
                        breadcrumbs swept away

Cold Spring Harbor

Today I celebrate
the joy of sunbursts
through the lace of trees,
an air of butterflies
played on a summer dulcimer,
a glissade of geese
on the deep blue waters
of the harbor.

It is my birthday and
life surprises me,
hides the future in a cloud.

But for this little while,
let the frog sing
his rapture in my ears,
let the sun smooth
gold upon my cheeks,
let the cool grass
stain my feet.

YOU ARE NOT ME

You Are Not Me

that is diversity enough

it matters not that burkas hide your body
while mine lies almost naked on the sand
or that, conversely, you can read
the waves of desert lapping at your doorstep
while I expound on Eliot and Twain

it matters not that your repast is spiced with cumin
or that your fingers bleed with pomegranate juice
nor does it matter that I shun the rain
while you, hands cupped to heaven,
gather drops rarer than black pearls

you are woman, just like me
that is unity enough

like earth our bodies open to man's seed
most times in love sometimes in shame
and open again always in pain
mothers of our future selves
bearers of men

we know joy
the butterfly flutter of our babies' hands
as they grapple with milk-laden breasts
the murmur of brides' veils
as they set sail for life

we know sadness
when our men heed the steel hiss of swords
we know grief
when we wash their dead bodies with our tears

you and I are woman
that is enough

Louisa

1883-1906

Louisa was a farm girl
who loved the feel of earth
but when she heard young Charlie sing
she thought she was in heaven

her blushes caught his eye
when from the choir he glanced
it was not long until he came
a-courting for her hand

they married when snow crystals
hung in winter air
by the ruby light of fall
they cradled close their son

Louisa was a housewife
who loved her hearth and home
she washed   she cooked
she kept her baby safe

on a morning cold and gray
Christmas baking done
she cleaned the stove with kerosene
a dormant fire within

flames quickly leapt upon her clothes
they set the house ablaze
Charlie could not save her
she died within the day

alone Louisa rests
beneath the churchyard earth
two oaks to shade her slumber
her name etched on a stone

Charlie grieves upon her grave
many a day and night
but Sundays when the church bells ring
he does not sing again

Salud, Jamie

I raise the glass to my lips
tremble and drink
beneath me the earth
your bones in the darkness
quiet

the sun of the south
the cold of your grave
my life   your sleep

I remember our moments together
raucous and lusty vignettes
the bar, the porch, the fishing, the sea

with a reel and a line
and a fast racing boat
you went courting a sea maiden
iridescent and sleek

hold fast, hold fast
the blue marlin is yours
you've got her
you've got her

her strength made you weak
entangled your line
you struggled   held on to the rails
lost your balance   went over the side

like a lover she claimed you
lured you with a glint of her skin
pulled you down to her watery bed

Salud, Jamie

the sun of the south
the cold of your grave
my life   your sleep

Les Feuilles Mortes

leaves scattered against ashen skies
drift down the empty street
beggars shunned
by stone-lipped window panes
orphans teased by wind
into a somber waltz
they spin in a vortex
disperse
on a melancholy note

she raises the collar on her thin gray coat
holds it in place
with bare chilled fingers
her heels clicking on the pavement
words coming to life
tapped with conviction
on an old typewriter

she shivers thinking of
another day
another country

in the milk-white
light of an autumn dawn
warm from lovemaking
she steps on cold terra cotta tiles
walks to the silent kitchen
listens to the hiss of steam
breathes in the black strong scent
domestic bliss
that does not last the day

her heels click faster
memories swirl
meander
drift away

It's a Laura Ashley, You Know....

says she the nine year old
with cherub cheeks
and cherry mouth
in answer to my compliment
a pirouette envelops her remarks

"Of course," I hastily reply
and seek the comfort of
my less enlightened peers

we who have shopped in five-and-dimes
darned our socks in times gone by
follow the swinging of her hem
let out a sigh then sip our tea

Mary's Poems

for Mary Watts

spare words

lean words

whittled away

like Giacometti figures

standing together

dense with life

pared down

to essentials

carved

to perfection

It's So Quiet — But Then It Always Is, to Me

in memory of Mary Whitney

your words haunt me
with their plain-spoken truth

of your deaf world, closed
to your own soprano voice
to the trilling of a wren
its wings brushing
lilacs by your window

as you stroke silk fur
Peacho and Thistle purr
Holly barks
yet this symphony of love
eludes you

from a distance
we speak words
formed by hands and minds
we hear
each other's thoughts
as they race in cyberspace

your words comfort me
solace in stolen moments
of uncommon quiet

comfort to you
would be the sound
of my voice

like a movie special effects planes piercing steel and glass wounds in the side spurting pyrotechnic blood flames up against a perfect sky clouds of smoke billowing out pushing their way through narrow city canyons rushing river of dark ash thick with odor of death lives crushed two towers crashed to the ground black eruption sad destruction chaos despair anger and fear shattered dreams slow motion grief ghostlike survivors risen victims of Pompei dazed in the care of strangers sudden brothers of a cosmic family heroes with asbestos boots rising to their death in search of life human birds on fire falling into sacred ground descent into heaven martyrs of the freedom flag red white and blue sprouting out of the smoldering heap out of the broken heart of America one nation indivisible hope courage liberty harbors the light dark September morning cell phones tenuous links crackling messages of love final good-byes crash in Pennsylvania's fields clip the might of Pentagon's wings long day's journey into a dazed week sudden seismic shift nation united waving the flag American pride candle light vigils funerals masses grieving the missing lost bodies dust to dust ashes to ashes life lost life born life goes on with a hole in the heart with a hole in the skyline pick up the pieces by hand with a crane follow the leader president mayor father peace on earth stay close yearn for a mother's embrace for the dull knife of experience quotidian motions semblance of calm centered by turmoil one day at a time up and down the ladder of feelings elusive enemy wanted dead or alive patience endurance wage war to make peace soldiers blazing the night laying waste to a wasteland of mountains and deserts adding rubble to rubble rabble of infidel hordes unyielding enraged burning the stripes and the stars of the land of the free and the home of the brave stitching smiles from threads of pain seeking sustenance from humankind no more blacks whites all shades in between stealing sleep from troubled nights a time to weep a time to mourn a time to wake a time to sing of freedom and hope out of the depths of the earth the depths of the heart crescendos of crystalline notes rising to heaven higher and higher towers reaching the sky

In Her Grief She Remembers My Name

her husband's body
burned by flames of evil
lost beneath the
latticework of steel
and glass and brick
crumbled monoliths
reduced to hills of
metal ash and cinders

music fills the church
but there is no joy in song
only a cloud of sadness
of silence and of prayer

she kneels
flanked by her
twin-towered sons
remains of a day that
will not see the sunset
of their father's life

she smiles as widows do
head held high
eyes like vacant windows
jagged panes
open to the smoke
the black soot seeping
into wounds already
festering

friends   acquaintances
approach
touch her hand
kiss her cheek
I too share in this pavane
of grief and comfort
I reach for her embrace

I am speechless
she whispers my name

September Trinity

Eve
September 10, 2002

what will tomorrow bring
other than resurgent pain
flashbacks of fire
smoldering steel
rain
said the weatherman
thank God for that
we could not bear the sky
achingly blue
crystalline clear
shattered again

let the raindrops cry our tears
let the clouds express our grief
if thunder speaks
let it speak of
anger and resolve

Day
September 11, 2002

it does not come, the rain
that was to wash away the cinders
lodged beneath our eyelids
instead
a confusion of clouds
scattered in the cold, blue sky
a shroud stretched tight
across our brow

at ground zero
we pray, we wrap
a shawl of silence
round our wind-whipped hair
the dust of the dead
swirling at our feet

Night
September 11, 2002

flags stiff with wind
crackle their presence
like gunshots in salute
we sing of country
huddle for comfort on the green

out of the darkness
prayers spark like fireflies
candles flame
prick the smudged ink of sky
the stars perplexed
gaze at the earth
ablaze with hope
and humbly
dim their brilliance

We Are All Brave

we who reclaim our lives from
the death-like clasp of night

look into the face of life
bite into the soft flesh
of a warm peach
lick the salt sweat
off a lover's mouth
feel the silk
of a newborn's hair

we whose eyes answer
the insidious dawn

look into the face of fear
recoil at the cracking jolt
of a door slammed shut
close the vacant gaze
of a dead friend's eyes
murmur a prayer
with our blood-streaked lips

we are all brave

we whose arms cradle
the newly living
we whose arms carry
the newly dead

In Praise of Man

I
on a narrow road by a cross light
a child on a bicycle quivers
eager to move
her father stands beside her
as the light turns green
his muscles taut from
strength and love
spring into a loving arc
ease the bicycle
into the road
pink streamers flutter
in the wind

II
people file out of
church pews
one by one
making their way
to receive the sacrifice,
with power and grace
he steps aside
allows his wife, his children
passage to the altar
cocooned
between the Deity and him

III
he walks with the bearing of a lion
muscles straining under a sweat-stained shirt
jeans worn to a bleached blue sheen
he kneels, folds his
hardened hands
into the soil, plants kernels
of new life, roots his strength
deep into the moist earth
smiles at the hope of spring

Loneliness

let us consider then the nature of this pain
this compression of the heart from
      subjugation
            abnegation
                revelation

the waiting for a cataclysmic bang
      from within or
            from without
a resolution which can never come
      because inertia sets the course

the growing of a parasitic vine
      always gnawing
            always gripping
the recognition that its tight embrace
      becomes a suffocating vise

a circle
      no beginning and no end
            waiting to be severed or enjoined

a wandering wind
      over a prairie plain
            never still   never silent

let us consider then the nature of this pain
this depression of the mind from
      alienation
            desiccation
                sublimation

Stirring the Pot

on this frigid January day
I feed
for sustenance
endurance
to fill the cracks
to shore erosion
to dull the fury
waiting for the snow
to fall
waiting for the
nondescript turmoil
without and within
to come
bury
hush into submission
earth rocks trees
monoliths of strength
that nourish
stabilize endure
yet cannot rise
to save themselves
they cave crumble
sway and break
in an eternal cycle

Sometimes, Oh Lord

I look at mankind in the subway
or the bus
and wonder why there's sadness
all around

take the men
ugly faces, tired hands
nights of seamy passion
loneliness beyond repair
or the children
their vacant minds
reflected in their skin so taut
anger flashing in their eyes
sparking in their curls

and the women
take a look
take a good look
at the reluctant mothers of the world
who kicked their throne
like children in revolt
their crown and mantle cast aside
for the privilege of barrenness

sometimes, oh Lord
I wonder why you have forgotten them
have they deserted you
or have you so withdrawn your help?

what does it add to your grandeur
to know the bruises of the heart
the wasting of the mind?

Prayer

Our Father who art in Heaven

Father, what does it mean?
Loving, stern, controlling
Soft-hearted? How can you
Love me and the rest of the world?
How big is your heart?

Hallowed be thy name

Which name? God,
Spirit, Life, Goodness, Grace,
Love, Serenity, Fulfillment,
Light, Being, Truth

Thy kingdom come

Teach me Godspace for
I am rootbound
Breathe life into my
Hollow shell, let it sing
The song of resurrection

Thy will be done on earth, as it is in heaven

How shall I know? The world
Is noisy and your voice is
Gentle, I would like a sign,
But that is not your way

Give us this day our daily bread

Chocolate and strawberries too,
Please

And forgive us our trespasses

Quiet anger denies comfort
Numbs me to joy,
Doubt makes me stumble
Lose sight of your beacon light

As we forgive those who trespass against us

Let your smile within me
Rise to my lips as I speak
Let your love's warmth be felt
As my hands touch others

And lead us not into temptation

Through the blind maze of greed
And envy, wrap me instead
With maypole ribbons
Of hope and love

But deliver us from evil

Dance me into the light
Amen

Zebra Sky

sinewy bands
of ochre
alternate
on swollen flanks
of smoke-dark
sky
pregnant with the night

surreal
suburban sunset
cusp of reality
and dream
a breeze of tails
a whisper of hoofs
intimations of Africa

Sunset Swans

demure maidens
preen
behind tall curtains of
lace-fringed grass
feathered skirts
rustle
one by one
ease
into the bay

debutantes at a ball
glide
all in a row
billowing gowns
drift
like clouds of snow
sparkle
with iridescent drops
of jeweled sunfire

Wordsmith

in the heat of his forge
he hammers iron thoughts
into pliable forms
tempers them
in cool waters of reason
shapes anew
smoothes corners of polemic
sculpts tendrils of poetry
joins them
cast iron strong

If Once You Have Slept on an Island

inspired by Jamie Wyeth's painting of the same name

you will never lie
on soft beds of temptation
on crumpled sheets of lies
on woolen layers of doubt

you will understand
the secret longing of the waves
the rapture of a windswept hill
the searing truth of storms

if once you have slept on an island
you will know
that life and death
are one

Dusk Dreams

There is a ship goes back and forth
From island cliffs to mainland port.

Her mainmast creaks, her wood rails sigh
When winds whip port and starboard side.

The skipper's hand is strong and true
When tacking, heeling, heaving-to.

Though warm and broad his smile may be,
His pain is deep, just like the sea.

He lives his best at eventide
When work is done and cares aside,

He steps ashore and heads for home
Where by the fire he sups alone.

He sits and watches dusk enfold
The sea and sky with cloaks of gold.

The ship is moored, the sailor lifts
A frothy tankard to his lips.

He slowly sinks his eyelids low
And lets the mem'ries come and go:

Those other days, with younger sails,
The salty songs and racing tales,

The velvet skies with diamond lights,
The fogbound days and milk-moon nights.

And, oh the welcome of his dear
When all was still and she so near

To touch his body and his soul
She took him in, she made him whole.

She smiles no more, still it would seem
She lingers close, just like a dream.

And so he slips, one autumn night,
Into that dream, forever bright.

The dark now steals the island shore,
It hovers, beggars by the door,

It reaches corners, roof and beams
Then quickly rushes like a stream

To still the sounds. The embers die
And settle slowly like a sigh.

My Man, He Went A-Whaling

My man, he went a-whaling, oh,
My man, he went away,
To make his fortune sailing, oh,
He left my bed one day.

He left it cold, he left it bare,
The sea would have its way.
His arms were strong, his hair was fair
His mind I could not sway.

He heard the whales a-calling, oh,
He heard them night and day,
To ride the waves like sleighs on snow
I knew he could not stay.

He loved me far into the night
Together, heart to heart,
And when the sunrise gave us sight
How sad it was to part!

I had his child to rock and hold
Long on a summer's night,
And when the winter sun grew cold
I sewed by candlelight.

Then, one spring day, a ship's first mate
Came knocking at my door.
Without a word he sealed my fate,
His eyes fixed on the floor.

"God rest his soul," was all he said
And turned without a sound.
My man is gone, my man is dead,
The whales, they took him down.

And now my heart's a-wailing, oh,
My heart has gone astray,
My man he went a-sailing, oh,
My man he went away.

The Widow-Maker

wrapped in a spider web
of wool
she walks
her homespun skirt
rakes the sand
seals the breathing holes
of crabs

searching
for the absent ship
her eyes skim
over the viscous sea

the sky
wrinkled like an oyster
closes her world
inside a gray
translucent shell

a briny crust of silence
settles over the leaden sea
still she walks
numbed by a storm of pain
her young sons in her wake

If I Had Courage

If I had courage
I would live by the sea
on an island that's rocky
storm-lashed and free.

In a white and blue cottage
sitting high on a hill
the curtains a-flutter
back and forth on the sill.

I would lie awake nights
I would sleep in the day
I would drift with the tide
let go where it may.

To the sands in the south
to the cliffs in the east
in sweet solitude
there I would feast.

If I had courage
I would sail on the sea
to an island that's rocky
and take you with me.

About the Author

Eleanor M. Imperato holds a Bachelor of Arts degree in English from Marymount Manhattan College and a Master of Arts in Liberal Studies from New York University. She is the author of *La Sarta* (2005), a chapbook of poems written in remembrance of her mother. A freelance writer, she has published numerous articles and has co-authored several books with her husband, Pascal James Imperato. Their biography, *They Married Adventure* (1992), profiles Martin and Osa Johnson, wildlife photographers who achieved fame in the 1920s and 1930s. Eleanor is currently at work on her next book of poems which will blend memories of her early years in Italy with historical vignettes.